**ISLINGTO**

D0505344

BRAVADO

Scottee

# BRAVADO

A Memoir of Working-Class Masculinity

(1991 – 1999)

OBERON BOOKS
LONDON

WWW.OBERONBOOKS.COM

First published in 2017 by Oberon Books Ltd
521 Caledonian Road, London N7 9RH
Tel: +44 (0) 20 7607 3637 / Fax: +44 (0) 20 7607 3629
e-mail: info@oberonbooks.com
www.oberonbooks.com

Reprinted with revisions in 2017

A catalogue record for this book is available from the British Library.

PB ISBN: 9781786823342
E ISBN: 9781786823359

Cover design by Oberon Books

Printed and bound by 4edge Limited, Essex, UK.
eBook conversion by CPI Group (UK) Ltd, Croydon, CR0 4YY.

Visit www.oberonbooks.com to read more about all our books and to buy them. You
will also find features, author interviews and news of any author events, and you can
sign up for e-newsletters so that you're always first to hear about our new releases.

This play is dedicated to the men
who made me hate them.

# Contents

# Foreword

I don't like working-class men, I don't like being around them, especially when they are drunk. I fear their capabilities, their loose tongues, banter and fast tempers.

I don't like being on a train or bus, or waiting in public when groups of working-class blokes are present, I fear encountering football supporters, stag dos and lads on a night out – I worry what they might do to me, what they might say, what might happen – I fear potential.

I hate talking to working-class men, being in changing rooms or public toilets with them, going into boozers, greasy 'Spoons or DIY shops. Any space working-class blokes dominate creates a recognisable response of sweaty palms, my eyes darting around the room pre-empting danger and an umbrella of worry.

However, this fear isn't one-sided, it's a mutual fear. They fear me and my effeminacy. They stare, they point, they laugh and nudge each other. Sometimes they take photos of me, sometimes they chant insults or point me out of a crowd.

To complicate matters, I also love working-class men. I love their familiarity. I'm married to a working-class man and I'm sexually attracted to working-class men. I equally fear and love working-class men – I live with a complex version of Stockholm Syndrome or 'trauma bond' because of my historic violent encounters with blokes.

In 2016 I sat in front of my laptop and decided I would attempt to cleanse myself of this unearthed fear, dread, worry. I purged all of my early, formative experiences with working-class masculinity into a document. The result is my first text for stage.

*Bravado* includes four very graphic accounts of what happens when a child is subjected to working-class maleness in a cultural climate of aggressive and sensitive masculinity. It explores sexual and domestic violence, post-traumatic stress disorder, abuse and revenge. It's this reason why I urge you not to read on if you find these subjects unhelpfully triggering.

After making performance for almost ten years I knew I didn't or perhaps couldn't perform this one. To perform it offers the audience a get-out – they know I survive, that I live to tell the tale. I wanted to remove that comfort. My choice in not performing is also a reminder that this won't be, can't be and shouldn't be wrapped up nicely in an hour. This stuff is by no means resolved for me – there is no learning, no moral to the tale – it's still very much alive.

As I wrote the show, I fantasised about what it would do if performed by those I feared – men. How would I get men to perform it? Simple, you ask for a volunteer.

Cis men are socialised to be confident and dominant, and so are usually the first to come forward, to take one for the team, to lead, to overpower. *Bravado* is performed by a volunteer and to date that volunteer has always been a bloke.

Of the other two essays in this volume, Stewart Who?'s is a reflection on what happened when he put his hand up to volunteer at the opening of *Bravado*. Likewise, Jen Harvie's explores the concept of bravado itself, and its relation to nineties maleness and homosociality.

What you should know is that this work comes with a massive dead weight of familial guilt – the stories recounted are of family who have since changed their stripes, who have fought their addictions and demonstrated to me their capabilities of love, softness and affection. They have turned their lives around. But *Bravado* doesn't explore that, only because this text explores my world from 1990 to 1999.

It's important I mention that this work also comes with lashings of fear – I fear what might happen by putting my experience out there. I fear drawing attention to myself so men can see me plainly. I fear what the men in question might do should they find this text. What happens should they read the fact I've got brave enough to out them but not brave enough to confront them. This is how maleness and misogyny succeed: they live off our fear and off their potential – it's time to relinquish it.

This isn't an easy read for you or me.

You have been warned.

Scottee
August 2017

# Bold Love

## THE 1990S

What are the opportunities for men and boys – especially working-class men and boys – to express their feelings? Where are the role models? What were the opportunities and emotional contexts in the 1990s, the formative years of Scottee's youth? In August 1990, US President George Bush led coalition forces, including from the United Kingdom, into the Gulf War. It was a war of immediate propagandising images, with daily footage of action broadcast live, continuously, and effectively in celebration, militarising the television landscape of Scottee's childhood and the video landscape of *Bravado*, and mixing with other contemporary images of heterosexual male idealism that *Bravado* invokes, including *Baywatch*. After the Gulf War, it was finally recognised how many veterans experienced post-traumatic stress disorder, another feature which touched Scottee's life through his Dad who was stationed in the Falklands, Northern Ireland and Germany before the Wall came down, and whose own father and grandfather had also been soldiers. From 1990 until 1997, the British Prime Minister was John Major, one of whose defining features was a lack of public expression of emotion. But the decade also started with the 1990 World Cup semi-final of England versus Germany, when Paul Gascoigne famously and, for many, endearingly wept after receiving a yellow card that would rule him out of the final had England made it through. Following Diana's death in August 1997, the new, young Prime Minister Tony Blair stepped up, voice quivering, to speak the nation's grief and to claim her as 'the People's Princess'. Publicly, it was a decade marked by the compulsory machismo of Bush and the emotional rectitude of Major, but also the irrepressible emotions of PTSD and the emotional possibilities modelled, however briefly, by Gazza and Blair.

## BRAVADO

In this global, public context of turbulent feelings, Scottee's *Bravado* turns mostly to the domestic and neighbourhood scene of his childhood to explore bravado – the usually male swagger deployed to impress, intimidate, and therefore control other people, in particular Scottee himself as a child and adolescent. In *Bravado*, Scottee explores how bravado operates publicly in rank-pulling, and magnetically drawing together bullying gangs. He examines its violence in intimate situations including the family home, and the sexual encounters of two lone boys in the bin storage sheds. But he also acknowledges bravado's attractiveness in others and its desirability for oneself. This attractiveness is displayed in the charisma and vivaciousness of McNamara and Smith, the 'hardest boys' in Scottee's childhood gang, who are first to 'master a technique' of getting up onto the scaffolding on the estate, and who strut, swagger, and spit down on Scottee once there (p. 30). Bravado's desirability underpins the boys' use of banter and of soldier-like surnames, no first names – let alone infantilising nicknames or diminutives. Bravado's desirability informs Scottee's wish to remain part of the gang despite the others humiliating him, and to ascend the scaffolding himself, regardless of his 'puppy fat' and fear of being caught by his Mum (p. 30).

*Bravado* is an exacting indictment of the pervasive violence of the male-dominated, emotionally-constrained, homophobic culture in which Scottee grew up, and of the many ways that violence was embedded – or legitimated – in his everyday life, partly through the apparent banality of bravado, banal because it is 'just for show' or 'just for fun'. At the same time, *Bravado* acknowledges the proximity of bravado to bravery, their shared roots in the word 'bold', the thrill of bravado's audacity, and the frisson of becoming the subject of the show-off's attention. Bravado can be sexy.

Throughout *Bravado*, Scottee acknowledges his own – and others' – mixed feelings. The braggart demeans others, but his audacious performance is also enchanting. Scottee is frightened by McNamara but admits, 'I sort of fancy him for frightening me' (p. 31).

Feelings are strong but not fixed or static; fear connects to desire, shame to pride, and hurt to love. *Bravado* shows and emphasises the complexities of feelings, particularly male feelings.

As *Bravado* painfully reveals, the effects of heterosexual male bravado on Scottee have been, since his childhood, demeaning, punishing, and enduringly wounding. Nevertheless, he allows it its attractiveness and desirability because he has the bravery to acknowledge the many ways that he – and countless others – are caught up in and informed by the conditions, value systems, and pecking orders of their cultural contexts and everyday lives. Bravado is not only part of those other boys in the gang, O'Mally, McNamara, and Smith among them. It is not only part of 'them'. It is also part of him, Scottee. In allowing bravado its complexity, Scottee legitimates his own complex feelings towards it. He acknowledges the complex conditions and expectations that form, constrain, and sometimes damage boys and men and their emotional development. Scottee boldly demonstrates the range of feelings boys and men might legitimately express, and he encourages them to do so, to change expectations of themselves and their fellow men and boys, and to take responsibility for the violence of their behaviour, past and present.

*Bravado* also shows how social relationships – like feelings and genders – are also on a continuum. There is a homosocial camaraderie among the boys of Scottee's gang; they mimic each other's behaviour and all obey the dominant McNamara. This homosociality is valued, while homosexuality is not; O'Mally routinely curses Scottee with misogynistic epithets during their sexual encounters in the bin sheds, spits in his face afterwards, and threatens to kill him if Scottee reveals their secret (pp. 33-34). But in *Bravado*, Scottee draws the links between homosociality and homosexuality, connecting scenes of both through shared behaviours of entering forbidden areas (the scaffold, the bin sheds), showing off, spitting, and bullying. Like feelings, desire is complex. In the enlightened understanding of *Bravado*, masculinity is neither static nor one-size-fits-all; neither is sexuality.

Everyday sexism, homophobia, and bullying will be dismantled not only when they are made visible, as Scottee makes them here, and not only when their explicit and extremely violent forms are properly routinely condemned. To eradicate them properly, cultures and individuals must acknowledge our unconscious or implicit biases, the many ways we all contribute to perpetuating the violence. This is not to blame the victims. It is to sympathise, as Scottee does, with those many whose cultural contexts mean they will inevitably be caught up in and complicit with violence which damages themselves.

## CARE

The world Scottee depicts in *Bravado* is harsh. As the opening text warns, 'This show contains graphic accounts of violence, assault, domestic and sexual abuse' (p. 21). It is clearly a priority for Scottee to reveal that violence, to call it out, and to hold its perpetrators to account. Despite the violence of Scottee's experiences and feelings, *Bravado* also shows desire, care and love, and it performs care. The camaraderie of the boys in the gang is a kind of love. Scottee's Mum carefully salvages sandwiches from the pub for him and his childhood friend White, 'before the men could put their pissy hands over them' (p. 24). Scottee protects his baby brother with strength and tenderness in the face of their Dad's uncontrollable rage. The children in *Bravado* are undoubtedly vulnerable but also resilient and often emotionally intelligent. Scottee aims also to enact care for his audience and for the performer who speaks his show. Everyone is informed about the nature of the show. The volunteer is warned several times about the material they will perform. They are invited to take breathers, given water, paid £100, and invited to stay for a drink afterwards, an invitation which is also an opportunity for the show's stage manager to check they are ok.[1] Following a tirade of anger towards Scottee's childhood tormentors, the show's final line speaks of love: 'I want them to love me' (p. 47).

---

1    Stewart Who?, '*Bravado*: A Perspective', also in this volume. Also listen to my interview with Scottee, *Stage Left with Jen Harvie, episode 4*, https://soundcloud.com/user-148494537

The 1990s world Scottee displays was one of violence, especially male violence and homophobic violence. The present world which Scottee bring us up to is also one of violence. But it is also a world of love. Scottee boldly shows the love.

Jen Harvie
September 2017

# *Bravado*: A Perspective

I've known Scottee since he was a teenager, when he hit the London club scene as one half of Yr Mum Ya Dad. His discipline has evolved over the years and his work is always a wonder to witness. He boasts a fuck-you lack of vanity, embracing the grotesque, milking self-loathing and then letting it sour in the minds of his audience. That he does this with a showbiz grin or drag de Dada, makes it all the more punchy. We've worked together a couple of times and he's hilarious company, a consummate professional and an awesome talent.

## ARTISTIC IRRITANT

I booked tickets for his *Bravado* show at Camden People's Theatre with curious anticipation. Scottee's chubby effeminacy left him oppressed and ostracised while growing up. Ironically, the gay scene wasn't an entirely loving sanctuary either, once he escaped the trials of home.

His angry drag, strident activism and music hall camp has often proved rather unsettling for some quarters of the LGBT 'community'.

## BUTCH BALLOON

Perhaps that needs clarification; Scottee is a fabulous artistic irritant to the men that value masculinity over sanity, sex over politics and hierarchy above everything. While puncturing that butch balloon, Scottee's also happy to stab at the racism and misogyny found lurking in some ashtrays of the drag scene. He was, and continues to be, a damn welcome court jester, happy to skewer the privileged queens.

Rage fuels much of his work, but a witty approach tends to leave you haunted, not irked. Yet his righteous fury seems absent in person. In private, he'll breezily scoff at macho posturing like it's a pathetic joke. Except we know it isn't. Patriarchy is not a joke. And it isn't funny.

## THE SHOW

It was a full house and the stage manager announced to the audience that a volunteer would be required. Nobody offered. She asked again. The silence was tense, seemingly lengthy and still, nobody waved a willing limb. Then, my hand went up.

'How hard could it be?' I thought, hoping my support would not only be fun, but speed up proceedings. I was taken aside and instructions were whispered. Foolishly, my imagined theatrical support was akin to a magician's assistant. Debbie McGee to Paul Daniels or Scrappy to Scooby Doo. I'd pictured a fleeting step into the limelight before returning to the cosy darkness, seating and wine. Except, the job at hand proved much bigger and far deeper.

## FIGHT OR FLIGHT

Every night a volunteer is asked to stand in front of the mic and read Scottee's script from a teleprompter. From the offset, all participants are warned that the material may be triggering for some, as it documents abuse.

Slowly, it dawned on my galloping brain – Scottee wasn't going to be in the show. The show was going to be me, reading his memoir of a north London childhood to the assembled audience.

It became clear with nuclear impact that this wasn't gonna be jolly, and the weight of responsibility became multi-tiered and complex. I didn't want to let Scottee down, nor disappoint the assembled audience. It helped, possibly, that the material has a grim familiarity. Scottee grew up on a council estate, part of an Irish family ruled by booze and violent chaos.

## FAMILIAR STORY

My family is Irish. I was raised in social housing. Violence and alcohol prompted my family's emigration from Ireland to London. By all accounts, it was a life or death transfer. Oh, and like Scottee, I'm attracted to men, fuckwits that they are.

It was a challenge to know how to pitch the script appearing in VHS-ish digital form on the screen before me. My purpose wasn't to dazzle, but to share Scottee's story. I made a conscious decision to read clearly, without drama and to find and inhabit his rhythm.

## KILLING BULLIES

A weird, almost professional calm descended. It was just me, the teleprompter, Scottee's story and my imagination. When he lost a fight because he didn't know how to punch, I was there. It was me. When he attempted to kiss his abuser, but was denied romance or control. I was there. It was me.

When he grew up, fled and flourished, I did too. When he still dreamed of killing his bullies, the dream was shared. Hating them, but desiring them? It was me. The cuts are deep and hard to heal. They're mine too.

## NOT A MUSICAL

The show is divided into three 'acts' with an Oasis song played between each excerpt. The instructions encouraged the narrator to sing along if they wished. I can't sing, don't like Oasis and didn't want to turn this dark episode into Lidl does Pop Idol. I didn't even sway to the blokey Brit pop, but I clocked a few in the audience who couldn't help themselves.

After the performance, a stage manager guided to me to a private room for a chat. I asked her, 'is this the live version of – if you've been affected by issues in this broadcast, here are some numbers to call?'

It was. Thankfully, I wasn't traumatised by the experience, but transformed in an indefinable way. I'd accidentally stumbled into somebody's pain and shared it with strangers by making it my own. The audience wasn't entirely strange. I was there with my partner. There was an ex-boyfriend in the audience and a couple of friends. This only added to the oddity. What had they thought, watching me read Scottee's graphic flashbacks, with its litany of blood, spunk and bile? Could they tell, could they read me, when the text struck a nerve? Did it speak to them too?

## DESCENT OF MAN

*Bravado* is a bold concept. It's an artistic howl, a cabaret of revenge, an evolving poem of grief that's unique at every performance. Each volunteer who voices Scottee's story will bring another angle and invoke another tone. The power of the piece is that whoever takes the mic, the story stays the same.

Abuse, physical or mental, leaves lasting scars.

Men are usually the perpetrators, but also the victims, and its inevitable cycle runs the world. Bullied kids turn on themselves. Drinkers beget addicts, punchers produce fighters and anger swells in the damaged hearts of survivors. *Bravado* hits you with this sick set-up, then spits you into the night to ponder your part in the circus.

Stewart Who?
March 2017

Bravado *is performed by an audience member. They volunteer to do something others wouldn't do. This is to demonstrate the act of bravado in the room.* Bravado *is performed in male space or reappropriated male space – pubs, garages, changing rooms. Three screens are placed in view of the audience. An additional screen in the audience is intended for the performer to read dialogue – hereby known as PERFORMER SCREEN.*

*This script is written as the text would appear on the screen.*

*Walk-in song: 'Bitter Sweet Symphony' by The Verve.*

## WALK-IN SCREEN:

BRAVADO

A memoir of working-class masculinity

(1991 – 1999)

## OPENING PREPARATION TEXT:

This show contains graphic accounts of violence, assault, domestic and sexual abuse.

Leave the room whenever you like, stay at your own expense.

This isn't a show for those of you still processing abuse.

We require one volunteer to perform this show.

You will need to be comfortable performing material about sex, violence and abuse.

You'll be required to read and sing along to a few Oasis songs.

Put your hand up now if you'd like to volunteer yourself.

*(Volunteer is chosen by technician.)*

## PERFORMER SCREEN:

Hello! Thanks for volunteering to perform *Bravado*. If at any time you want to pause or take a breather please put your hand in the air so the technician can see you.

You will read forty minutes of text, the screen will change once you've read everything on that screen.

You will be paid one hundred pounds for your time.

If you fluff your lines that's totally okay.

The material you'll be performing is of a graphic nature – you are going to talk about domestic abuse, sexual violence and the extremes of bullying.

To indicate you are okay with this please give the technician a thumbs up. If not please return to your seat, we totally understand.

*(Pause for confirmation.)*

There are three Oasis songs to perform. You'll sing along to the originals so don't worry if you are not the best singer.

Take a deep breath. You'll be ace.

There is a bottle of water on stage for you.

Thank you and don't forget to wait around so we can pay you and buy you a bevvy!

Scottee. X

*(During this time a rewinding of the imagery used in the show, including date markers, flashes past on audience-facing screens, similar to VHS rewinding.)*

*('BLOOD' appears on all screens.)*

## BLOOD

I can tell you what the inside of every
pub in Queens Crescent, Kentish Town
and Camden Town looked like.

I can tell you where pubs once stood, what they were
called, who ran them, who sat where and even what
some of the houses above a few of them smelt like.

*('1991' flashes up on one of the audience screens.)*

I come from a family of drinkers.

Now, you might be painting a picture
of a family of Irish alchie winos.

That would be wrong.

Only half my family are Irish.

We're well-turned out, Nan calls
us 'respectable people'.

My family are like all the other families on the
estate – they worked hard and played harder to
forget Monday would soon be upon them.

The men prop themselves along the bar –
told off by the Mums for using
grown-up language in front of us kids.

The women, our Mums, are sat at tables with
packets of Brannigans Roast Beef and Mustard
flavour crisps, torn open for sharing.

We are left to play outside with one pound coins
jingling in our pockets, given to us by drunken
relatives or by even drunker friends of relatives.

Our spends are spent on sixty p. cones
of chips swimming in vinegar and if you
were lucky a screwball from the Greek ice
cream bloke who often held the cone and
your hand for just a second too long.

The once-thick carpets are rough and smell of
stale beer and cheap air freshener bought from
Gordon & Ruth's Home and Hardware.

On a Sunday the landlady would put
freshly cut sandwiches on the bar.

Salmon paste smothering cheap, white, thinly cut
bread that instantly became stale at the edges.

Mum would wrap a few up in a kitchen towel for
my friend White and I, sending us out before the
men could put their pissy hands over them.

White and I spent many afternoons and
occasional evenings outside The Napier.

The Napier was known as my Mum and Dad's pub
– they didn't own it, it was just where they drank.

The Gypsy Queen, Robert Peel and The
Shipton were my Grandad's haunts, the Lion
and Unicorn or the Spread Eagle my Dad's,

The Carlton was my Uncle's pub.
My other Uncle drank in Hackney.

The Dragon was a bit different – a pub for
everyone and the only pub my Nan would step
foot in, suitable for women of a certain age.

The Napier had two rickety picnic benches and
a four-foot high concrete mound outside of it.

The cement had set a long time along,
no one knew why it was there – it just was.

Sometimes it would be White's island, other
times we'd both just run up and down it passing
the time and trying not to cut our knees.

White would often get her yellow, floral
summer dress dirty. She was the sort of girl
who sat open-legged sipping Orangina,

…telling me how to climb the willow tree across the
road, never conscious you could see her knickers.

The drunk adults would encourage us to call
each other girlfriend and boyfriend.

We wanted to be friends,
they wanted us to be something else.

This dynamic would eventually mean we
would never see each other again.

The concrete mound was our boundary
set by my Mum – beyond it were a row of
three semi-demolished terrace houses.

Bricks and broken glass sit amongst used needles
with speckles of dried blood in them.

We're told to stay away from these mysterious
objects because we would get AIDS.

If a fight kicked off at The Napier (which
inevitably it did) men always took their violence
outside at request of Mrs McCarthy.

From on top of our concrete hill we'd watch men
battle out old grudges and new with their fists.

Most ended before they started but there
would almost always be blood spilt or
spat on the pavement we played on.

*('1994' flashes up on one of the audience screens.)*

One night outside The Carlton my mate's Dad and
some known bad guys from our estate got into a scuff.

Hearing the breakout my friends and I run down
Grafton Road only to catch the last part of the fight.

I often turned my head away when I knew
something nasty was going to happen.

As I turned back I spotted my Uncle in the
fight, his opponent was covered in blood, as if

he'd been drinking watered down ketchup and
it had all slid down his cheeks and chest.

When someone is bottled the sound of
the breaking glass stops everything,

everyone's shouts and jeering immediately
subside to an ordered angry murmur.

It's the thing you knew you could do but should
never do has been done, and people are in
shock, disappointment, the crescendo.

Once that bottle breaks across someone's
body, like the last orders bell, it instigates
a frantic, silent, kerfuffle.

*('1993' flashes up on one of the audience screens.)*

The first time I got punched in the face was outside
Lyndhurst Hall – the social club on the estate.

A new boy on the estate, Carr had moved
down from Newcastle with his Mum.

He was knocking about on his own;
we suspiciously approached him.

He sounded different, he sounded
like the kids off Byker Grove.

We let him play out with us and took the piss
a bit at the way he spoke behind his back.

O'Mally somehow orchestrated a situation in which
I had supposedly insulted the newcomer's Mum.

We already knew this was dark.

Dark was something we said to each other if we
knew our boyish banter had entered no-go territory.

'Don't be dark' was our way of
saying enough is enough.

Replicating late-eighties teen films the boys
circle us both and egg us on a fight.

Wanting to prove his worth on new turf
he goes along with O'Mally's lies.

Knowing I have no option I try to recall everything
my Dad had taught me about fighting.

Arms up, thumbs out, close your mouth.

I half-heartedly swing and miss.

Carr swings back, he hits me on the side of my head.

I'm stunned someone would actually do that
so he takes his opportunity to hit me again,

and again,

and again.

Each time the circle comes closer and each
time I miss my opportunity to hit back.

The boys become quieter with every punch.

A rage builds inside me – it's anger,
frustration and fear in equal measures,

my eyes well up so much so that I don't
see the next punch before it's too late.

He backs off with his arms tightly
poised either side of his temples

– someone has taught him how to fight.

The boys change their focus from silently
critiquing Carr's ability and start staring at me.

I taste my lips and instantly recognise
the warm, metallic taste of blood.

Everyone stops; including Carr
who stares blankly at me,

no sign of remorse as he throws his torn
white vest into the grass, the only thing I
managed to destroy in our scuffle.

He reveals his milky, rippled stomach,
spits on the grass.

Tears run down his chiselled cheeks, he is
crying in silence, awaiting my next move.

I stare at his feet, trying not to be caught
looking at his half-naked body.

Carr has bust my lip and my nose,

both are forcing blood down my neck,
disappearing under my t-shirt.

The rage in my body subsides and I stand
there not knowing what to do next.

Miller slaps him on the back to congratulate him.

McNamara pulls me by my collar and
throws me outside of the circle;

I fall over, pick myself up and walk towards home
never looking back at the circle of friends.

I ring the bell to get into our block.

Mum takes ages to answer the door.

Dad sits me down on the kitchen table and says
I'll get more than a fat lip in my lifetime.

Mum puts TCP on my cuts, TCP is the
answer to most things in our house.

I'm told to calm down,

stop crying,

be brave.

I sit on the toilet with the door locked and light off.

Like Carr I begin to cry quietly whilst Mum
and Dad watch *The Generation Game*.

*Song #1: The performer sings 'Champagne Supernova' by Oasis.*

*('SPIT' appears on all screens.)*

## SPIT

Long summer evenings,

the sort that seem to last longer than the
summer holidays evoke memories of spit.

…other people's spit.

*('1996' flashes up on one of the audience screens.)*

I'm about eleven when our estate
is done up by the council.

We, the Crescent Boys,

our self-given title named after the area we live in,

full of bravado and Doner meat adopt
the scaffolding as our stomping ground,
our adventure playground, and our boys club.

It takes McNamara and newcomer Smith, the
hardest boys in our gang, no time to master a
technique of getting up to the first platform.

They are thin and already have developed muscles.

They slide their hands into their grey jogging
bottoms whilst they wait for us to join them.

The challenge has been set.

It's almost as if we only ever climb things
to reassert our place in the group.

I, as ever, struggle to pull my puppy fat over the bars,

that and the fear of being caught by
my Mum are holding me back.

Determined to fit in and avoid effeminising
myself further I push harder,

I begin to sweat and panic more.

O'Mally, Miller and Smith are
now all on the scaffolding,

Each pretend to help me, offering
their hand just out of reach.

I'm surrounded by the noise of almost
fifteen other teenage boys from my estate
trying to climb up the cold metal poles.

The scaffolding smells like my Dad when he
comes home from work. Rusty and dead.

I'm-half ignoring them but still hoping they'll reach
down and pull me up without anyone noticing.

All four begin to rain spit down on me, laughing
through pursed lips, egging each other on.

McNamara hacks up phlegm but it's a lucky near-miss.

Their dehydrated saliva is so thick it changes the
colour of my Coconut Joe t-shirt from the market.

I'm now determined more than ever
to reach the first platform.

With a fuckload of frustration I leap
and manage to pull myself up.

I regain my breath, slightly fucked from the exertion.

O'Mally, Miller, and Smith's sniggers fall
silent when McNamara says 'allow it'

(that's council talk for 'leave it').

The boys back down, he is harder
than them all put together,

…he is chunky but with biceps,
he is thicker set than us all.

He frightens me.

I sort of fancy him for frightening me.

He has sex – so we're told, daily.

He has got two girls pregnant, already.
This is seen as an achievement of his ability to…

a) ejaculate and b) get a woman to have sex with him.

O'Mally talks about how big his cock is to
counteract McNamara's admissions.

O'Mally is aggressively competitive.

As we sit on the platform, watching the
sun go down on our estate, we start to
talk about what we'll do tonight.

I wipe the spit from my hair casually as if
to throw my tight auburn curls back from
my forehead, ignoring its wetness.

I look to the sky and say something like 'it's raining'.

I'm making excuses for their nastiness,
ignoring the obvious and protecting
myself from another dose of shame.

Although this seems submissive, it's actually
an act of defiance, it's self-preservation.

O'Mally thinks he has the better of me,
he does but he doesn't.

A few years after this my relationship
with O'Mally intensifies.

*('1999' flashes up on one of the audience screens.)*

From about the age of fourteen, instead
of now openly berating me, O'Mally
organises times when we're alone.

Once out of sight from our block he instructs
me to go into the bin storage sheds in
various other blocks across our estate.

Once he has me in there he routinely turns off the
lights, locks the door and approaches me slowly.

*(Five second gap.)*

It's pitch black.

He reaches down my jogging bottoms
and I'm ready. I know the routine.

Again his dominance prevails; he has chosen when,
the location and how it will happen
– it's all on his terms.

My back is always against the wall.

O'Mally fumbles clumsily to be erotic,
just sort of rubbing my hips as if we were in
an eighties movie without any of the dry ice,
mood lighting or romantic dinner.

Every time I attempt to kiss him he
turns his head away from my lips.

I kiss his sweaty neck instead, avoiding
the black dirt living in the creases of his neck fat.
He isn't from the cleanest of homes.

We both ignore the smell of other people's rubbish.

I want him to want me, but this is functional for him
– emotionally he is absent from our transaction.

Once he is ready he guides my head towards the floor.

Whilst giving him head he calls me
things like 'bitch' and 'whore'.

I develop a way of using my spit to clean
his foreskin before giving him head.

Our encounters never last long.

*(Ten second pause.)*

He forcibly cums in my mouth. I spit his spunk on
the slippery, painted Camden council grey floor.

I use the inside of my t-shirt to wipe off his excess.

I use the cold, sweaty, breeze brick wall
to support me to stand up.

Once on my feet, stood in front of
him, O'Mally spits in my face

– making the act of oral sex not one of
teenage experimentation but one of violence,
aggression, control and power.

He says: 'Never again, tell anyone and
I'll kill you, understand me?'

I say nothing; I know it's a question
I don't need to answer.

This isn't a threat but a promise.

I'm unable or perhaps unwilling to see
the power I have over him.

He thinks he has the better of me,
he does but he doesn't.

He uses the light of his Nokia to
find his way out of the shed.

He closes the door behind him and walks
off into a cold, foggy, silent Sunday.

I use my sleeve to wipe his spit off my face, my Mum
is phoning me repeatedly, it's past my curfew.

I sit in the dark until I hear the heavy
security door of the block slam shut.

I close the shed door and finish myself off in silence.

I walk home, apologise to Mum, get in the
bath and close my bedroom door.

*Song #2: The performer sings 'Stop Crying Your Heart Out' by Oasis.*

*('TEARS' appears on all screens.)*

## TEARS

Everyone is drunk and being just fourteen
I'm allowed a few Smirnoff Ices.

*('1999' flashes up on one of the audience screens.)*

Mum doesn't want me to end up
like her, afraid of alcohol.

She grew up in a house where alcohol
was feared and misused.

Because of this I'm periodically allowed
to drink with Mum and Dad,

…not in a middle class way – you don't drink
with your dinner. This isn't an education
in getting drunk, it's a facilitation.

You drink to get drunk.

You drink to forget what life is like, what it
used to be like, what it's likely to be.

After a heavy evening of drinking, going from
cans to shorts, Dad goes to the toilet.

Almost immediately my Uncle starts
calling my Mum fat, indirectly.

Feeling awkward, uncomfortable
and unsure I leave the room,

Having parents who booze means you fear the
unpredictability of their drunken states.

You fear the potential.

You begin to create the possible fallouts,
how you might defuse this one without
getting caught in the middle, again.

You begin to shake nervously, fearing the unknown.

I loiter in the hall.

*(Ten second gap.)*

I want Dad to walk into the banter to rescue
Mum with his wit and dominance,

I also want him to stay in there until it breezes
over so it doesn't erupt into a brotherly fight.

Dad is still in the toilet – he is taking his time.

As Dad opens the toilet door I tell him
what is going on. I tell him he has to do
something, as Mum will be really upset.

He pushes me against the cold plastered wall
where the notice board lives. Takeaway menus
and photobooth cut-outs fall to the floor.

I call for my Mum.

He's saying something like 'Do you want some, then?'

Actually, I'm not sure what he said, this just
sounds like a thing my Dad would say.

His grip around my neck becomes tighter. It's
at this point I realise it's not a mistimed joke.

I don't recognise the man strangling me.

I divorce the idea that my Dad is doing this
to me; he has done it before, I know he
doesn't mean it. I know it's not him.

He clips my cheek lightly with a soft fist.

Like a Dad punch but with some
emphasis and thought behind it.

My Mum realises what's going on.
She runs into the hall. My baby brother
begins to cry from his room across the hall.

Dad's hands are forcibly removed from my
throat whilst he repeats 'Yeah? Yeah? Yeah?' With
one fell swoop he knocks Mum out the way.

My Aunt and Uncle leap off the sofa and are
pushed into the table in the living room.

Through the meandering hall I catch his
eye, my brother at this point is clinging onto
my leg, crying through his dummy.

I pick him up, run into my parents'
room and push the lock across the door,
knowing this will give me some time.

I barricade the door with a pine chest of
drawers Mum bought in Camden.

I remove the linen from the far-right-hand drawer
beneath the bed and put my brother inside it,
closing it gently, leaving enough room for air.

I don't want my brother to witness this.

He does as he is told.

The white, heavy door is being kicked repeatedly;
this isn't the first door I've seen him try to kick in.
However, this is the first one that's solid wood.

I imagine what's happening on the other side
as I slide down the chest of drawers;

using my weight against it I stop him from getting in.

I plan if I should jump out the window,
whose door I might knock on.

Shame keeps me rooted behind the door.

*(Ten second silence.)*

I'm not worried they'd kill each other –
they never do, they know when to stop hitting
each other, they love each other too much.

The thumps, swearing and smashes begin to fall
silent, like a drum kit that's been pushed over.

The cymbal finally settles and the
obligatory crying begins.

I get closer to the door to hear muffled talking
intercepted by gasps for air and more crying.

Mum pleads with me to open the door. I refuse.

She continues to plead with me.

I ask her to promise me he hasn't got a knife.

Dad pleads with me to believe her, knowing
at this point I won't believe him.

I can hear my brother being unusually silent.

I push the drawers back and unlock the door with
my foot behind it should I have to jam it shut again.

I'm ready to push back. I've pushed Dad
before, the countless times I've thrown myself
between Mum and Dad on a Friday night,

Saturday morning or Sunday afternoon
if the benders lasted that long.

Dad has some cuts to his head and
cheek, they are both crying.

I relax, I know it's over.

Crying often means the end of the night – my
family seem to cry when they can no longer drink.

Crying immediately after a fight isn't because
they are sorry, it's embarrassment.

Embarrassed that yet again we're sweeping
broken glass or boarding up smashed windows.

That yet again the neighbours will know.

That it will be my turn to fend questions
from the boys on the estate.

All of us live in homes with booze,
conflict and/or drugs.

I push the chest of drawers back, the door swings
open fully of its own accord, and it reveals destruction,
pain and the aforementioned embarrassment.

I take my brother out of the drawer, no one
questions why I put him in there, no one asks.

I rest him on my hip, give him his dummy and wait.

As a family we sit on the bed as my Aunt and
Uncle leave, slamming the door behind them.

Dad comforts my brother whilst apologising
for ruining another Christmas.

I tell him it's okay and that I know he didn't
mean it, I make excuses for him.

I want it to be a normal Christmas so ignore
everything that has just happened.

Dad says he doesn't know what came over him.

I empathise. I tell him it's not his fault.

I know all too well this is what running away
and into the army has done to him.

What giving a child a gun has done to him.

What losing friends, gunfire and fear have left him
with even though he has never spoken of it.

What being asked to kill or be killed has done to
his and countless other Dads' mental health.

The effects of a disciplinarian, Edwardian
military father who saw battle and
bloodshed – the son of another soldier.

I tell him it's not his fault.

I feel sorry for him.

A logic that perhaps only the children
of addicts understand.

*Song #3: The performer sings 'Don't Look Back in Anger' by Oasis.*

*Potential*

*I want to fight*

*I want to kick back*

*I'm fucking resentful*

*('CUM' appears on all screens for longer than expected.)*

## CUM

Whilst walking up the escalator at Euston station,

failing to attempt to sneak past a drunken
stag do wearing a baby pink raincoat,

Ten men in a slurred chorus of

'you fat gay, you fat gay' in blokeish harmony.

*('2016' appears on one of the audience screens.)*

It was ten-thirty pm; the station was typically quiet in
sound but still populated with hundreds of people.

However all you could hear was the sound of train
announcements and the echo of their insults.

Every commuter on that escalator ignored
the chant directed at me, as if they had
heard it to be their imagination.

To pretend it wasn't what it was
is easier than showing alliance.

Instantly my body fills with rage – anger,
frustration and fear in equal measures, a
toxic concoction I've felt before.

*('1993' appears on one of the audience screens.)*

I'm immediately thrown back to that first
fight – it's them against me and no one
in the fucking station has my back.

I say nothing and wait for the brow
of the concourse to appear.

Something or someone else distracts them.

I stand at the top of the escalator
greeted by two armed policemen;

they are talking to each other, scanning
the crowd and ignore my blank stare.

I walk to the exit closest to my house and my
eyes begin to fill like they've done before.

I want to punch something and I don't know why.

I'm resentfully thrown back to those long
summers lost in heavyset maleness.

*(Ten second pause.)*

Recently, I saw O'Mally and McNamara for the first
time since I ran away from home almost a decade ago.

I've never set foot back into Queens
Crescent, it's home of my entire trauma,

going back only brings back bad memories,
it's the site of too many unrecorded,
unwitnessed and unconfessed crimes.

They both hadn't changed, except they were fatter.

McNamara's once-thick-set neck on a
triangle, tapered torso has disappeared.

O'Mally's face now dominated by a purple
scar running from brow to jaw.

We've aged but we haven't changed.

Perhaps our bruises are just more visible.

McNamara points at me speeding
past on my red, glittery bicycle

'…look who it is, Bruv.'

As I speed past I catch a glimpse of their laughter.

They are still bound by bravado and brotherness.

They have each other.

They're laughing at me again.

I cycle faster to catch up with my heartbeat.

That snapshot of one laugh reminded me of
all the shit men have put me through.

And so I begin dreaming my revenge.

*(Ten second silence.)*

I wanted to cycle back towards them,
ask them what they are laughing at.

I want them to feel inferior to my
new-found confidence.

I want to surprise myself with my
new-found confidence.

I want to kick them, I don't know why
but that feels like a good start.

I want to kick them until their ribs are bruised to fuck.

I want to punch them with my fists until their eyes
water and they cannot see me throw the next punch.

I want to spit in their face and create
empty threats that bind them in fear.

I want to repeatedly spit at them from a great
height, laughing as I humiliate them.

I want to grab them by the collar and throw
them to the floor, out of the circle.

I want to frighten them, for them to live
with the fear I know too well.

I want to out them to their families and tell
them about our shitty sexual encounters,
not just with O'Mally but with the rest that
remain unnamed in this memoir.

I want to use their real names.

I want to humiliate them about the size of their
cocks and the fact they cum all too quickly.

I want to strip them of all of their
heterosexual, male confidence.

I want them to cry behind closed doors whilst
*The Generation Game* blares out down the hallway.

I want them to feel sore, hurt and bruised
– physically and emotionally.

I want to bottle them, make them
bleed in front of their friends.

I want to scar them, I want to be the one who reminds
them who I am every time they look in the mirror.

I want them to sit behind a door
worrying if they've got a knife.

I want to take a knife, pierce their skin, puncture
their stomach and let them taste the metallic
grit of their own blood on their lips.

I want to taunt them, bully them and
leave a lasting effect on them.

Pollute their lives with trauma that will
forever watermark their confidence.

I want them to stay awake in bed at night wondering
what they'd do if they had access to me again.

I want them to plan their revenge on me.

I want their revenge to be bloody, ugly and resentful.

I want them to second-guess if they should be brave
enough to tell the world what men have done to
them in case those in question come after them.

I want them to feel guilty for telling the truth
knowing that some of this stuff isn't their fault.

I want them to worry even in their awakening.

I want them to feel so disgusted with
their gender and its capabilities,

…its potency and dominance, that they
shudder every time they are called a man.

I want them to feel everything I've
felt but this time by my hands.

I want them to acknowledge I exist,

…that I survived scathed, bruised, battered, bleeding.

I want their mental health to be unpredictable,
aggressive and time-consuming.

I want their confidence to be in crisis,

to feel they are not good enough
and that they do not belong.

That they will never belong, that they
will never be good enough.

I want them to acknowledge that they can
see me, all of me and that they are too
scared to tell anyone what they see.

I want them to drag their baggage kicking
and screaming into their thirties, out of
the nineties and into every friendship
and relationship that comes after it.

I want them to be frightened of me.

I want them to be frightened of men.

*(Five second silence?)*

I want them

I want them to fuck me

I want them, to want to fuck me

I want them, to want me, to fuck them

I want to choke them with my cock – wilfully and
begrudgingly. As act of my love and hatred of them.

I want them to stare at my bulge when I slide
my hands into my grey jogging bottoms.

I want them to fantasise about me in their
deepest, darkest teenage wank fantasies.

I want them to watch porn so they
don't have to think about me.

I want them to secretly stare at my dick.

I want them to desire me.

I want to cum in their mouths and
I want to spit in their faces.

I want them to wank in the dark, alone.

I want their lust for me to be
complicated, ugly and ignored.

I want them to be full to the brim with
shame, trauma and oppression.

I want their sexuality to be informed by
the violent acts I force upon them.

I want them to find me on Facebook, to look through
the images of my children's birthday parties, holidays
in Spain and drinks with the lads at the estate.

I want them to be deeply jealous of the fact
I still have friends from our childhood.

I want them to be angry that I have no
recollection my actions live on in their life.

I want them to envy how easy it's been,
how my violence has meant I've gotten
everything I've asked for.

How being a straight man has meant I win.

Repeatedly.

I want them to be like me.

I want them to like me.

I want them to die.

I want them to be sorry.

I want them to leave me alone.

I want them to love me.

WWW.OBERONBOOKS.COM

Follow us on www.twitter.com/@oberonbooks
& www.facebook.com/OberonBooksLondon